MW01247760

IN GOD
THEY
TRUSTED

T. Diana

in Jesus' love,

Pete Marshall

Feb '93

IN GOD THEY TRUSTED

David Manuel
Peter Marshall

Photography by David Manuel,
and on pages 24-26 and 56,
by Bruce Allen

Published by
Crossroads Christian Communications, Inc.
Pittsburgh & Toronto

Printed and Distributed by
Paraclete Press, Orleans, Massachusetts

Acknowledgements

The authors wish to acknowledge their
appreciation for the contributions of:

Rosemary Carroll, and the interpreters of Plimoth Plantation

Francis Labovites, Creative Color of Cape Cod, Massachusetts

Hobart Caywood, Superintendent of the Independence National
Historical Park, Philadelphia

Paraclete Press, printer

and Fritz Klein of Springfield, Illinois, for his indelible
portrayal of Abraham Lincoln

Credits

Quoted material is excerpted from *The Light and the Glory*. Copyright © 1977 by
Peter J. Marshall, Jr., and David B. Manuel, Jr. Published by Fleming H. Revell
Company. All rights reserved. Used by permission.

Duotones on pages 22, 23, 28, 29, and 47, courtesy of Library of Congress;
Paintings on pages 11, 15, and 18, courtesy of Pilgrim Society,
Plymouth, Massachusetts;
On pages 40 and 41, courtesy of Valley Forge Historical Society;
And on page 46, courtesy of New England Life Insurance Company.

4th Printing

© Crossroads Christian Communications, Inc. 1983
Box 8000, Pittsburgh, PA 15216
Library of Congress # 83-61973
ISBN: 0-919463-07-X
All Rights Reserved
Printed in the U.S.A.
By Paraclete Press, Orleans, Massachusetts

To all who gave their lives
that America might become
''One nation under God,
Indivisible,
With liberty and justice
for all,''
this book is dedicated.

Foreword

In the summer of '81, *100 Huntley Street,* our daily Christian television program from that address in Toronto, undertook an unprecedented broadcasting venture called "Salute to Canada." In thirty days, we traveled across Canada from sea to sea, originating live from twenty-five different cities, and judging from the response to it, it did much to promote unity in the Body of Christ in Canada.

But long before, I had been given a special burden for the United States. It had come to me, as I stood on the steps of the Lincoln Memorial, pondering an invitation from Thomas Zimmerman to host a television series, produced by the Assemblies of God churches in the United States, of which Dr. Zimmerman was General Superintendent. It was then that the Lord impressed very strongly upon me that I was also to carry a burden for America, a nation which He had raised up to be a Christian beacon. Standing there, in front of the memorial to perhaps the most revered President in America's history, and looking out at the Washington Monument pointing to heaven, and the dome of the Capitol in the distance beyond, I sensed deeply that the destinies of our two countries were somehow combined, and that somehow we would be given an opportunity to bless the United States.

Some time later, when Billy Graham was a guest on *100 Huntley Street,* he seemed to enforce that conviction, when he said: "I believe that Canada stands in a unique position. If Canada should have a spiritual awakening and a revival, the whole world would look to her." It was not to get the world to look at Canada, but to encourage the world to look to Christ, that we began producing Christian programming in French,

Greek, German, Ukrainian-Russian, Italian and many other languages, and making it available in foreign lands, as well as airing it at home. We also made it a continuing policy to encourage all our viewers to pray for global crises, wherever they occurred.

The spiritual awakening in Canada has begun, and as for relations between Canada and the United States, the time has come to emphasize the positive. Thus was the concept for a Salute to America born. What better way to express our gratitude for, and spiritual kinship with, our brothers and sisters south of the longest undefended border in the world, than to broadcast a special daily Salute, live from Washington, D.C., for the week of the Fourth of July.

Barry Armstrong, who heads our U.S. ministry, has caught the vision. So has David Manuel, who had written the book with me on Salute to Canada. We now asked David to script a Spiritual Heritage segment for each of the five programs we would do. We also asked Peter Marshall to be involved in the narrating of these segments and to help introduce them on the air. The son of the late Senate Chaplain and of author Catherine Marshall, Peter had often been a guest on *100 Huntley Street,* and I greatly admired the stirring and challenging book that he and David co-authored — *The Light and the Glory,* which traces God's hand in the founding of America. Barry would produce the segments, and to direct them, who could do better than Bruce Allen, who had done such a fine job on similar segments for Salute to Canada.

But I also wanted to offer our friends in the States something that would commemorate our new Salute — something truly unique, that they would treasure.

This handsome volume with its on-location photographs is the result.

We hope that you will enjoy it, that it will touch your hearts as it has ours, and that it will inspire you with the example of the faith of some of the men and women who first set America's course.

—David Mainse

David Manuel and Peter Marshall

On location.

Bruce Allen and Barry Armstrong

One Small Candle

In the fall of 1620, a small but determined band of Christian men and women set sail from England, to find a new way of life in the New World. These Separatists (as they were called for having separated themselves from the Church of England) had already lived together as a church for a dozen years in Holland. Now they felt God calling them to America, where they were to live in Christian love, and by their example help others to do the same. They had no idea what to expect, other than Indians and wilderness, but as their leader William Bradford would write, "they knew they were Pilgrims, and looked not much on those things, but lifted their eyes to heaven, their dearest country, and quieted their spirits."

They sailed in a hired ship called the *Mayflower* — 102 of them crammed into a below-decks space about the size of a volley-ball court. There is a reproduction of the original *Mayflower* anchored in Plymouth harbor, Massachusetts, where visitors can get a feeling of what that voyage must have been like. The living conditions were so cramped that there was scarcely room enough to sleep. Nor could they cook anything. They had one kettle over a carefully guarded fire, in which they could boil water to soften the dried peas that were part of their staple diet.

But that wasn't the worst part; they had been delayed by foul weather and recurring problems with a sister ship, the *Speedwell*, which never did sail, and by the time they left, the winter storm season was upon them. That meant all passengers were ordered below, and all the hatches were battened down, and for sixty-six days, as

The Mayflower *in heavy seas.*

they were beset by one gale after another, no one was allowed topside to get a breath of fresh air, or to lean over the lee rail. It all took place below, with the little ship rolling and pitching and yawing, people being sick, children crying, only two lanterns to give any light, and not even enough headroom to stand up straight.

Yet the Pilgrims did not despair. They had already weathered many hardships together, and they had learned to let adversity draw them closer together than ever. Now their leaders sensed that God had allowed the storms, to temper them in the refiner's fire. And so they prayed, and their spirits lifted, and to the utter amazement of the ship's crew that had to be on deck in the storm, above the howling of the wind *singing* could be heard below decks!

At last the storm abated, and land was sighted — the wind-swept dunes of Cape Cod. They had been blown far north of their intended destination in the Virginia territory, yet they took this as a sign from God, and gathered on deck to give thanks for His having delivered them from the raging Atlantic. For only one of their number had perished in the crossing, at a time when such voyages often took the lives of at least half the passengers on board. God had called them to be one, and to love and care for one another, and they had learned new depths of trusting and caring during their two-month ordeal.

The tempering of the Pilgrims now entered its second phase. For as they gazed upon the bleak and desolate shore of Cape Cod, the full impact of being "strangers in a strange land" sank home. As Bradford described it: "All things stand upon them with a weatherbeaten face; and the whole country, full of woods and thickets, represented a wild and savage hue. . .what could now sustain them but the Spirit of God and His grace?"

But that was enough. For they had come in obedience to His call, and were now prepared to trust Him implicitly. They sent a search party in the ship's boat, called a shallop, to find a suitable site for the settlement, and they sailed around the inner perimeter of the Cape, until a sudden storm broke their rudder and sent them scrambling ashore for their lives. That night and the next they sheltered on a little island, and when at last the storm broke, and the day dawned fresh and clear, they discovered that they were in a natural, deep-draft harbor that could easily accommodate the *Mayflower!*

Moreover, when they rowed to the

mainland, they found a God-given site for settlement — on a gently sloping hillside, which ran down to the shore and would be ideal for drainage. They also found *four* fresh-water springs, and best of all, the surrounding land had already been cleared for planting by some Indians that had apparently vanished.

Rejoicing, they went back to fetch the *Mayflower*. Soon they drew up the plan of the settlement, of which the modern "Plimoth Plantation" is a faithful reproduction. First came the common house, to shelter the women and the sick, and then came other houses, and finally the block house at the top of the hill, where they would worship and gather for defense, in case of an Indian attack, for the Jamestown colony in Virginia had been repeatedly embroiled in fights with the Indians.

But this construction took time, and there was no time. The captain of the *Mayflower* had agreed to keep his ship in the harbor to provide some shelter, but

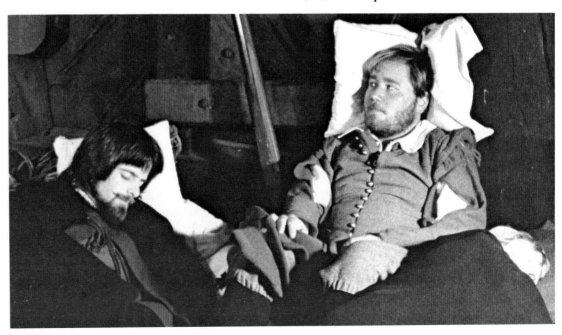

The Mayflower
wintering over.

winter was hard upon them now, and a hard winter it was — far more severe than any of them had ever experienced, or prepared for. And so, they worked in desperation to erect permanent, heatable shelter. The men, already weakened by the voyage and inadequately clothed, caught colds, and kept on working, ran fevers, and kept on working, and finally caught pneumonia and began to die. Fully half of their small band would die that winter, and at one point there were only five men well enough to man the guns, if it ever should come to that — which by the grace of God, it never did.

For the nearest Indians turned out to be friendly, and were in turn well-treated by the grateful Pilgrims. The first Indian, Samoset, walked right into the settlement and down the main street to the common house, where the men were gathered in a meeting. Knocking on the door, he greeted them in perfect English, and soon introduced them to a Patuxet Indian named Squanto, who had already spent a number of years in England, first as a captive and then a visitor, having recently been returned home by some friendly explorers.

When he got back to his homeland, he discovered that his tribe was gone, and he was bereft, until the arrival of the little band of praying English families. It was obvious that they would not survive the winter, and so he adopted them, teaching them how to catch eels and fish, and most important, how to grow the Indian's winter food, corn. Squanto literally saved the remainder of the Pilgrims, and they

Falling sick.

thanked a loving God for sending him, along with Massasoit and the Wampanoags, without whose friendship they might never have survived.

With the coming of spring, the iron grip of winter loosened on the earth, and green shoots sprang up in the wake of the receding snow. The time of tribulation was over. God now honored the obedience of the Pilgrims by blessing their crops and giving them an abundant harvest. To celebrate, they decided to have a time of Thanksgiving, and invited their Indian friends to join them. But when chief Massasoit arrived with ninety braves, the Pilgrims were first stunned — it would take all their winter provisions to feed them — and then relieved, for their guests had brought with them enough game to feed everyone for several days. That was the

Planting corn.

*Squanto and
Edward Winslow.*

*The first Thanksgiving
(Courtesy of Pilgrim
Historical Society)*

"All things stand upon them with a weatherbeaten face...."
—*Governor Bradford.*

first of many Thanksgivings that the Pilgrims would observe, out of gratitude for all that God had done for them.

Burial Hill overlooks the town of Plymouth and its harbor. There is an exceptional sense of peace there, where the Pilgrim Fathers are buried. John Howland's grave is there. His epitaph reads: "Here ended the pilgrimage of John Howland. . . . He was a godly man, and an ancient professor of the ways of Christ." And William Bradford, their beloved leader for thirty-five years, is also buried there. They are gone now, but their legacy lives on — for their church became the model for all the Puritan churches which soon followed, and their civil government

also became the model for the earliest form of American Democracy.

But most of all, they demonstrated in their lives that it *was* possible to live together in Christ, trusting and obeying Him — an example which has quickened the hearts of Christians the world over. In the words of William Bradford, looking back at their experience: "As one small candle may light a thousand, so the light here has shown unto many, yea in some sort to our whole nation. . . ."

A City Upon a Hill

"Land ho!" came the cry from the crow's nest, atop the *Arbella's* mainmast.

"Where away?" called the captain, standing by the helmsman on the quarter-deck.

"Two points off the larboard bow!"

These last words were lost in the commotion of the passengers rushing to the fore-deck, as they strained to catch their first glimpse of land in months. And sure enough, there on the hazy, sunny horizon, a blue-green band began to appear. An hour later, the firs of the rock-bound coast of Maine could be seen. John Winthrop, their leader, shook his head in wonder; never in his life had he seen pines as tall as these, shimmering almost silver in the afternoon sun. He took a deep breath and could smell their scent. What an adventure they were embarked upon!

For them, it had been two years in the planning, ever since the installation of William Laud as Bishop of London had made it impossible for Winthrop and his friends to purify the Church of England from within. The Puritans, as they had come to be called, wanted to remain loyal to the Church; they did not want to separate themselves, as the Separatists had before them. But Laud and the other bishops saw no need for such purification, and made life exceedingly unpleasant for those who practiced it — to the point where they felt that the only way they could fulfill their mission would be by personal example, at a safe remove, three thousand miles away. Accordingly, those who were prepared to go, got their families ready, sold their lands, and insisted upon Winthrop becoming their governor, before they set sail.

It had been a peaceful crossing, for the

Governor Winthrop drafting "A Model of Christian Charity."

Atlantic was as calm in late spring as it was storm-tossed in late fall. A couple of weeks earlier, in late May of 1630, John Winthrop had sat down in his cabin, and taking pen to paper, summed up the significance of their adventure:

A Model of Christian Charity

Thus stands the cause between God and us: we are entered into covenant with Him for this work. . .to follow the counsel of Micah, to do justly, to love mercy, to walk humbly with our God. For this end, we must knit together in this work, as one man. . . . We must delight in each other, make one another's condition our own, rejoice together, mourn together, labor and suffer together, always having before our eyes our Commission and Community in this work, as members of the same

*For Puritan children,
God was at the center
of their lives, even
when learning the
alphabet.*

A — In ADAM's Fall,
We finned all.

B — Heaven to find,
The BIBLE mind.

C — CHRIST crucify'd,
For Sinners dy'd.

D — The Deluge drown'd
The Earth around.

E — ELIJAH hid,
By Ravens fed.

F — The Judgment made
Felix afraid.

G — As runs the Glafs,
Our Life doth pafs.

H — My Book and Heart
Muft never part.

J — *Job* feels the Rod,
Yet bleffes GOD.

K — Proud *Korah's* Troop
Was fwallow'd up.

L — *Lot* fled to *Zoar*,
Saw fiery Shower
On *Sodom* pour.

M — *Mofes* was he
Who *Ifrael's* Hoft
Led thro' the Sea.

N — *Noah* did view
The old world & new.

O — Young *Obadias*,
David, *Jofias*,
All were pious.

P — *Peter* deny'd
His Lord and cry'd.

Q — Queen *Efther* fues,
And faves the *Jews*.

R — Young pious *Ruth*,
Left all for Truth.

S — Young *Samuel* dear,
The Lord did fear.

T — Young *Timothy*
Learnt Sin to fly.

V — *Vafhti* for Pride,
Was fet afide.

W — Whales in the Sea,
GOD's Voice obey.

X — *Xerxes* did die,
And fo muft I.

Y — While youth do chear
Death may be near.

Z — *Zaccheus* he
Did climb the Tree,
Our Lord to fee.

body. So shall we keep the unity of the Spirit in the bond of peace. . . . We shall find the God of Israel is among us. . . . He shall make us a praise and glory, that men of succeeding plantations shall say, "Lord, make it like New England." For we must consider that we shall be as a City upon a Hill. . . .

No sooner had they dropped anchor in the harbor of what is now Salem, than they immediately set to work, borrowing heavily from the experience and organization of their Pilgrim cousins, some sixty miles down the coast. They worked hard — so hard, in fact, that they soon earned a reputation which has survived to this day, as the progenitors of the Protestant Work Ethic. But those modern authors, who tend to cast them in the currently accepted stereotype of somber, sin-obsessed killjoys, overlook the fact that they also played hard. Indeed, there was such balance in their life, that work often seemed like play, especially when it was done together, as it often was, in cooking bees, sewing bees, husking bees, quilting bees, and the like,

A colonial spelling bee.

with spelling bees for the children, for the Puritans put a high value on education. And when a Puritan farmer was building a barn, it was a festive time for the whole community, with the wives spreading a magnificent outdoor banquet for the men, once the roof was up. In fact, "raising the roof" became synonymous with having a first-rate party. Witness the town clerk's description of a dinner held in celebration of the dedication of the new Lynn meeting-house in 1682. So many guests were invited from surrounding towns, that the only place large enough to hold them was a barn, from which the cattle and chickens had been removed. The trouble was, the chickens kept flying back in, and roosting on the rafters over the heads of the dinner guests, much to the dismay of the Lynn pastor, Mr. Shepherd.

> Mr. Shepherd's face did turn very red, and he catched up an apple and hurled it at the birds. But he thereby made a bad matter worse, for the fruit being well aimed, it hit the legs of a fowl and brought him floundering and flopping down on the table, scattering gravy, sauce and divers things upon our garments and in our faces. . .this did not please some, yet with most it was a happening that made great merriment.

In addition to such merriment, however, there was also decorum; for instance, when there was courting to be done, the young man would come calling with the whole family present, for the Puritans had a well-defined moral code — and hardly any divorces. In sum, they intended their whole lives to glorify God, and they felt that they were establishing a Bible Commonwealth for this purpose. Christ was to be the center of their lives, and the church was to be the hub around which their town re-

volved. In fact, Puritan farmers were not allowed to set up a new settlement in the wilderness, unless that would-be town were first incorporated as a church, with elected elders and ordained pastor, approved of by the other pastors of the colony.

For two generations, the Puritans cleaved fairly close to this ideal, most of them regularly asking God to show them wherever they had strayed from His path, and what they needed to ask forgiveness for. And as long as this attitude continued, God honored their obedience and blessed them mightily, with bountiful harvests, flourishing trade, and prosperous shipping. Meanwhile, the Puritans taught their children all the skills that they had been forced to learn in a hurry — how to build, make, design or repair practically everything they needed for working and living. Houses, barns, tools, furniture — they could do it all. And with God's help, they could do it well — so well, in fact, that a young Puritan family, just starting out, needed only their hands and their health, plus an ax, a gun, a plow and an animal or two to pull it, a wagon, a few tools, and some cooking utensils. With these, they could carve out a homestead anywhere.

And they did, no longer bothering to form into churches before going into the wilderness, and no longer bothering to travel the increasingly longer distances to get to church on Sunday. For there was one thing that the first generation had neglected to teach their sons and daughters, the most important lesson of all: total dependence upon the grace of God. They themselves had known the absolute necessity of this, through the overwhelming adversities that they had overcome, and they had demanded as much of themselves spiritually as physically.

But when God began to pour out His blessings upon those who had so faithfully trusted and obeyed, they grew complacent. They began to relax their standards, no longer requiring of their children what they had hitherto required of themselves. As a result, with each successive generation, there was more self-reliance, and less reliance on the Lord. And with self-reliance and prosperity, came greed. Where once three acres were deemed sufficient to support a family, now thirty acres were not enough, and soon it would take three hundred. In the words of the great Puritan preacher, Cotton Mather: "Religion begat prosperity, and the daughter devoured the mother."

As one pours over the diaries and letters and sermons of these later generation Puritans, one can sense God calling them back to Him. There were plagues of grasshoppers and caterpillars, and droughts of increasing severity, yet nothing seemed to reach them — until finally, in 1675, God allowed the one thing they all feared the most to come upon them: a massed Indian uprising. The little village of Deerfield was massacred, and the list of towns similarly obliterated grew rapidly — Swansea, Taunton, Dartmouth, Middleborough, Groton, Lancaster. . . .

As reports filtered back to Boston, the people who had taken church for granted, or stopped coming altogether, now in panic flocked to their churches for guidance.

Indian attack.

28

Puritans going to church.

They called on their ministers to declare a day of fasting, humiliation and prayer — after all, it had worked before in ending droughts — and the ministers did as they were asked, though the older ones predicted that it would take a far deeper repentance to move God's heart now. And they were right. No sooner had the people emerged from their day of fasting and prayer than fresh word was received of more towns falling under the tomahawk and the torch, and of relief columns being ambushed.

Now the people were desperate, and their pastors recommended that nothing less than a wholesale renewal of their church covenants was needed. And so, all over New England, congregations met together and renewed their covenants with God and with one another, repenting individually and corporately, and reconciling relationships that in many cases had been broken for years. They humbled themselves and sought His face and turned from their wicked ways. And God heard,

and had mercy, and gradually the tide of battle turned in favor of the beleaguered colonial militia. The chastisement was lifted, peace was restored, and their land was healed. And now they did what they had not done in so long: they gave thanks to God. The Puritans had learned a lesson that they would not soon forget — at least, not for another generation.

Today, we Americans owe a great debt to the Puritans, not only for the Congregational Church system and our town meetings, and most of the basic tenets of our social morality, but for the fact that our nation was established as a republic, a constitutional democracy under God, ruled by law, and not by the whims of popular fancy.

29

One Nation Under God

Philadelphia — the name means "City of Brotherly Love," and in 1740, it appeared to be just that. The reason was the radical message of a preacher named George Whitefield — America's first great evangelist. So popular was he, that he had to preach out-of-doors; no church could hold the thousands that flocked to hear him. So he stood on the steps of the old courthouse, and with much enthusiasm began to exhort the multitude which had come from miles around to hear.

It was not the first time that vast crowds had come to hear Whitefield. A close associate of John Wesley's at Oxford, he had experienced a dramatic conversion to Christ and had gone to bring the message of Salvation to the coalfields of Bristol and Gloucester. Miners by the thousands gathered in the fields on their way home from the mines, to hear something that no one had ever told them before: Jesus Christ loved them, and had given His life for them, that their sins might be forgiven, and they might have eternal life. As they listened, white gutters began forming on coal-blackened cheeks, and more and more came to hear, until one periodical estimated the largest crowd at 23,000!

The Wesley brothers had come to America before Whitefield, and had urged him to join them. But soon after he had, they had grown discouraged and returned to England. Not Whitefield, however; he stayed, and began riding up and down the Eastern seaboard, preaching at every opportunity. His message was so simple that it appeared revolutionary, in that it did away with the abstract, calcified theology which had come to clog man's communication with God. For Whitefield said that

Independence Hall.

Salvation was available to anyone, highborn or low, self-righteous saint or miserable sinner.

And what must one do to be saved? Just ask God's forgiveness for your sins, known and unknown, accept Christ as your Lord and Savior, and turn your life over to Him. A simple choice, yet the most important one a man could make — and it had never been put that simply to Americans before.

George Whitefield's arrival coincided with a tremendous revival that had suddenly broken upon New England like a lightning storm upon a parched land. It started in the town of Northampton, Massachusetts, under the preaching of the prominent theologian, Jonathan Edwards, who preached on the reality of Hell and startled his parishioners into considering the hereafter. From there, it spread like wildfire, from town to town, coming to be known as the Great Awakening. And the lightning rod which carried it the furthest was Whitefield. They said that he preached with the power and authority of one of the old Apostles, and wherever he preached, church records show that revival broke out.

Thus did he come to be standing on the steps of Philadelphia's courthouse, and looking out over the several thousand people who had dropped tools and pots and had hurried to hear him, he raised his eyes to heaven:

"Father Abraham!" he cried out. "Whom have you in heaven? Any Episcopalians?"
"No!" shouted Whitefield, answering his own query.
"Any Presbyterians?"
"No!"
"Any Independents or Seceders, New

31

Sides or Old Sides, any *Methodists*?"

"No! No! No!"

"Well, whom have you there then, Father Abraham?"

"We don't know those names here! All who are here are *Christians* — believers in Christ, men who have overcome by the Blood of the Lamb, and the word of His testimony."

"Oh, is that the case? Then God help me, God help us all to forget having names and to be *Christians* in deed and in truth!"

Standing in the crowd that day was America's foremost scientist and best known publisher. He was fascinated by the effect that the message was having on its listeners, and by the extraordinary projection of the speaker's voice. Retracing his steps back down Market Street until he could no longer hear the preacher, Ben Franklin calculated that in an open space,

Franklin and friends.

his words could be clearly heard by 30,000 people!

Each day that Whitefield returned, so did Franklin, who recorded: "It was wonderful to see the change in our inhabitants! From being thoughtless or indifferent about religion, it seemed as if all the world were growing religious, so that one could not walk through the town in an evening without hearing psalms sung in different families of every street."

Franklin befriended Whitefield, and the two became close, though in all of Whitefield's subsequent visits to Philadelphia, he could never persuade his learned host to give his heart to the Lord — at least, not then.

By 1776, Philadephia had become the capital of the Continental Congress, and in early July, the momentous event in American history took place there. Delegates from each of the thirteen colonies had gathered in solemn assembly, to decide once and for all whether they would break with Great Britain and become the United States of America.

British Customs agent.

It was a decision that was being undertaken with great reluctance, for a number of the delegates were believing Christians, as were many of the people they represented, and they wrestled with the question of whether God's Word condoned what they were considering. The thirteenth chapter of Paul's letter to the Christians in Rome was explicit: believers in Christ were to come under their civil authorities, as if God Himself had placed them in that authority.

On the other hand, many Christians were convinced that "resistance to tyranny was obedience to God." And there was no denying that they were being subjected to

*In this room, on
July 4, 1776...*

*The Continental
Congress first met in
Carpenter Hall.*

tyranny. After having been allowed to govern themselves and run their own affairs for a century and a half, suddenly they were being taxed oppressively, denied representation in Parliament, and refused rights that were basic to all Englishmen since the signing of the Magna Carta.

Moreover, the Colonists had sent appeal after appeal to their king, only to have their appeals mocked and spurned, despite the fact that their cause was being championed in Parliament by two of the great statesmen in British history, William Pitt and Edmund Burke. And now they had just learned that George III had refused to even look at their latest appeal. Perhaps the more fervent Patriots among them were right, when they cried: "No King but King Jesus."

Certainly the majority of the pastors in America agreed with them. Throughout the land they were calling upon their flocks to remember the mission which had brought the Pilgrims and Puritans to these shores in the first place: to live for God's will, as He had called them to do, and to create a Christian commonwealth, based on His laws. And the text that they most often preached from was Galatians 5:1, "For

freedom Christ hath set you free; stand fast, therefore, and do not submit again unto the yoke of slavery."

Even so, each delegate had to make his own decision. And they knew, that if they did declare independence, they would bring down upon themselves the mightiest military power on earth, in all its force and

*"A silence fell
over the room. . . ."*

*With quills such as
these, a nation came
into being.*

*The first site of the
U. S. Supreme Court*

fury. Only the sheer grace and mercy of God would prevent them from being overwhelmed. They also knew that the British were notorious for their ruthless suppression of insurrection. If they lost, America would be reduced to one vast penal colony, and every delegate in that room would be hanged for treason.

As the hour drew near for the final vote, the delegation from Delaware was deadlocked. The man who could break the deadlock was spurring his horse through the night, trying desperately to reach Philadelphia in time to cast his vote for independence. This was Caesar Rodney, and his own case was especially poignant, for he had cancer of the face, and had been about to sail for London, where there was a surgeon who had had success in treating cases such as his. By casting his vote for independence, he was voting his own death warrant, yet not for a moment did that thought slow him down. He rode through the woods at the height of a storm, as he had never ridden before, forcing his horse through creeks swollen from torrential rains.

At length, as the delegations were about to be polled for their votes, the doors burst open, and Rodney was carried into the chamber. He was exhausted, his clothes mud-spattered, a scarf covering his disfigured face. But he was in time. His vote broke the Delaware deadlock, and inspired several other delegations as well. The rest of the colonies followed suit, with only New York abstaining. They had voted to become one nation under God.

When the roll call was completed, a silence fell over the room. The late afternoon sun cast its soft rays through the tall windows, falling on a brass candlestick,

a carved eagle over the doors, a pair of spectacles lying on a polished desk. The magnitude of what they had just done, and what they had committed their country to, sank in.

Some men, like Witherspoon of New Jersey, bowed their heads in prayer. Others gazed out the windows, tears in their eyes, as they saw the dark clouds of war that could soon engulf America. John Hancock finally broke the silence: "Gentlemen, the price on my head has just doubled!"

There was laughter, and then Samuel Adams arose: "We have this day restored the Sovereign, to Whom alone men ought to be obedient. He reigns in heaven, and. . .from the rising to the setting sun, may His kingdom come."

Independence Hall was the site of another event of great historic significance, which took place not long after freedom from Great Britain had been won. And in the

light of the role Ben Franklin played, one wonders if his heart might not have been touched by his friend Whitefield's message, after all.

It was 1787, and delegates from the thirteen new states had gathered for the Constitutional Convention, to work out the grounds on which they would become a nation. But things were not going well. For in order to establish a viable national government with a Constitution that would work not just now, but in the future, the States were being called upon to relinquish some of their sovereign rights, to create — and come under — an authority greater than themselves. And that they did not want to do. Contention reigned, to the point where the New York delegation had already gone home in disgust, and others were about to follow suit. Hardly anyone present believed that they would ever agree on anything conclusive, and assumed that the dream of a Union of States was just that — a dream.

It was at this crucial moment, that America's most renowned agnostic, now 81 years old, rose to speak. The room was hushed.

> In the beginning of the contest with Britain, when we were sensible of danger, we had daily prayers in this room for Divine protection. Our prayers, Sir, were heard, and they were graciously answered. All of us who were engaged in the struggle must have observed frequent instances of a super-intending Providence, intervening in our favor. . . . And have we now forgotten this powerful Friend? Or do we imagine we no longer need His assistance?. . . I therefore beg to move that, henceforth, prayers imploring the assistance of Heaven and its blessing on our deliberations be held in this assem-

Liberty Bell.

bly every morning, before we proceed to business.

The assembly was stunned. No one spoke, while all considered what he had said. Franklin's speech marked the turning-point in the deliberations. From there on, progress was made, States set aside their pettiness and opted for the greater whole, and the Constitution — and the United States of America — came into being.

39

The General

Courtesy of Valley Forge Historical Society.

He sat astride the big gray horse and drew his greatcoat closer about him; the snow was blowing almost laterally now, across the frozen terrain. Before him, his men filed past in a ragged column of fours, leaning into the wind. They were silent as they passed, and he was silent, too, making no attempt at hearty words of encouragement. He was there, and they knew he cared. And he did — he could see how few had adequate protection, how many were ill-clad and without boots. He could see the bloody footprints in the snow.

Eleven thousand men trudged past him that morning, on their way into Valley Forge. Two thousand of them would die of exposure and illness that winter of 1777-78, in the harrowing, tempering experience that came to be known as America's "Crucible of freedom." Yet the army survived, and emerged the following spring as hardened steel, never to be defeated again. Historians have called it a miracle and credited George Washington with holding the army together and thus preserving America's freedom. But the General gave the credit to God.

They say that you can tell a great deal about a man from his home, and Mount Vernon was very dear to Washington's heart. He had spent many happy years as a child here and later acquired it by inheritance. He kept a greenhouse filled with citrus fruit trees and other exotic plants that friends who knew of his interest in botany, would send him. From the broad, columned verandah overlooking the Potomac, to the formal gardens and the long sweep of the driveway where you can imagine a coach-and-four turning in, there is a serenity that makes you want to linger as long as possible. It reflects the peace that was in its owner's heart.

Mt. Vernon

Sadly, the General had little time to spend at his beloved Mount Vernon. For he had committed his life to public service, not as some do today, for personal gain or aggrandizement, but as a servant-leader, in the footsteps of Him who said, "I am among you, as he who serves." He left home in 1755, as an intrepid young colonel, going off to serve under Braddock in the Indian wars. His mother had sent him off with the prayer: "Remember that God only is our sure trust. To Him, I commend you," and she added, "My son, neglect not the duty of secret prayer."

He did not neglect it; he copied prayers from the Book of Common Prayer into his field journal, and was later seen in private prayer by a number of his men. God did

preserve him in battle, and his personal bravery under fire rallied a faltering militia on more than one occasion, and became the stuff of legend. At the Battle of Monongahela, where Braddock was killed, Washington had two horses shot out from under him and received holes in his clothing from four different musket balls. Fifteen years after the battle, Washington and his close friend, Dr. Craik, were surveying in that Western Reserve, when they met the chief of the Indians who had fought against Braddock. Through an interpreter, the chief recalled the events of that day, and how he had pointed out to his warriors the tall officer riding out in front of his concealed troops:

"Quick, let your aim be certain, and he dies." Our rifles were leveled, rifles which, but for Him, knew not how to miss. . . . It was all in vain; a power mightier far than we shielded him from harm. He cannot die in battle. . . . Listen: the Great Spirit protects that man and guides his destinies — he will become the chief of nations, and a people yet unborn will hail him as the founder of a mighty empire.

As Washington grew in years, he became one of the foremost leaders in the Virginia Colony, a man whose dignity and wisdom befitted his uncommonly tall frame. He was a natural choice to represent Virginia at the 1775 Continental Congress in Philadelphia, and when it was decided that a commander-in-chief of the Continental Army must be appointed, he was again the logical choice. Modesty bade him depart that chamber at the possibility, at which John Adams wrote to his wife that he knew they'd found the right man. Washington accepted that assignment, as he had and would accept every call to public service, but he was faced with an awesome responsibility — not only to lead the army, but first to shape it into an army. For at the time he assumed command, it was a motley collection of hometown regiments and militia, with no experience under arms, not even among the officers, and no discipline. What he had was a gathering of individualists, who were expert riflemen almost to a man, and who were wilderness-hardened and ready to fight, but who had no training whatsoever, and had never in their lives let anyone tell them what to do.

Nevertheless, the General proceeded to bring order out of chaos. His first general order set the tone of his command:

The General most earnestly requires and expects a due observance of those articles of war established for the government of the army, which forbid profane cursing, swearing and drunkenness. And in like manner, he requires and expects of all officers and soldiers not engaged in actual duty, a punctual attendance of Divine services, to implore the blessing of Heaven upon the means used for our safety and defense.

That first year of the war, Washington fought a brilliant harrassing campaign, never strong enough to stand toe to toe with the British, but nevertheless, tying up vast numbers of their soldiers, and giving their general staff fits. Even so, it was the grace of God that even when defeated, they were able to "rise and fight again," in the words of General Mad Anthony Wayne.

Washington knew that it was God's grace which was preserving them, and frequently acknowledged their debt publicly. And after the miracle that took place on Brooklyn Heights, practically all

Washington takes command. (Courtesy of the New England Mutual Life Insurance Company.)

of the men under him were ready to acknowledge it, too. The Continental Army was trapped on Brooklyn Heights, surrounded on three sides with their backs to the East River, and all their reserves over on Manhattan. British warships hovered at the mouth of the river, prevented from sailing up it and drawing the noose tight, by a strong, steady northeast wind that had suddenly blown up and showed no signs of abating. Even so, with nothing but water at their backs, the army was finished, as soon as the British pressed home the attack.

But for some inexplicable reason, the British stalled — all the next day and into the night, though the Americans had only enough powder left to give each man two rounds. As it gradually became obvious that the British were going to wait until morning to launch their final assault,

Washington called a council of war and informed his generals that he had decided to attempt an evacuation by small boat, under cover of darkness. It appeared that the fleet had anchored for the night, probably to coordinate their movement with the land forces in the morning. Every small boat that could be found was pressed into service, and by God's grace, there were enough men in the army from Marblehead and Salem, who were expert small-boat handlers. These men had spent their lives on the water and knew how to move a dinghy or a dory through the water surely, and above all, silently. For the wind had died down now, and while the flat calm enabled the boats to carry more men, the slightest sound would give their maneuver away.

Long queues of men silently formed up

on the beaches and waited patiently for the boats to take them off (reminiscent of another miracle that took place at Dunkirk, two centuries later). Above them on the heights, Washington rode everywhere, making sure that the trenches were still manned so that the British would not suspect, repairing breakdowns in logistics and communications, and making sure that their desperate gamble kept moving.

Even so, it was taking too long. The first

shadings of pink were beginning to lighten the eastern horizon, and there were still three hours needed. In a few more minutes, the British would see clearly what was happening, the fleet would blow the small boats out of the water, and British Grenadiers with fixed bayonets would overwhelm those left on the heights.

British and American diaries recorded what happened next: a ground fog suddenly rose out of nowhere, and rolled across the river, blanketing everything on land and sea. Though the sun rose higher and higher, the fog remained — long after it should have been burned away. Finally, the fog shredded, and the British, realizing what had happened, ran to the shore and began firing, but the last boat was just out of range. Nearly eight thousand men had been extricated from death or imprisonment, and the American cause had been preserved, without the loss of a single life.

Yet the tempering of this army was still to come. That took place at Valley Forge, and Washington himself designed simple twelve-man huts which were dry, could be heated, and took no special skill to build, and which his men got up as fast as they could. But no design of his or anyone else's could stop the fever which reached epidemic proportions in the camp. On top of that, some States neglected to send supplies and provisions for their regiments; some of the suppliers under contract took the army's money, and then sold their supplies to the Redcoats instead, who paid in silver and gold coin, rather than nearly worthless Continental scrip. And all the while, Congress, having fled to York some sixty miles away, refused to believe Washington's reports of how bad things were, and accused him of exaggerating.

Huts at Valley Forge.

Parade Ground.

As the winter wore on, and nearly a quarter of their number had already perished, spies reported their enfeebled condition to the British, comfortably ensconced in nearby Philadelphia, and the prospect of an attack in force became inevitable. Freezing, sick, and nearly starving, the Yankees were in no condition to repel such an attack, and there was nothing to do but pray — pray and wait.

Washington prayed much that winter, for morale had sunk so low that many of the men no longer had the faith to believe in victory. But as long as they could see that their General still had faith, his faith would have to stand for theirs. And it did. Despite all the deprivations and misery, the army held together, when throughout history other armies in similar circumstances had simply melted away and dissolved, the men going back home to farms and jobs and families. But not these men, not when their General made a point of visiting each hut every day, to encourage them.

Washington Monument.

They stayed, and they became forged into steel in that valley, and the following June they fought the British toe to toe at Monmouth, and showed them a new breed of fighting man that shocked the British generals. Soon the Americans began to beat them at every turn, and finally at Yorktown resoundingly defeated their best field general.

At last, with victory achieved, a grateful nation unanimously insisted that their General become their first President. And in his Inaugural Address, he gave all the credit where it was due, and called upon his countrymen to do the same:

It would be peculiarly improper to omit, in this first official act, my fervent supplication to that Almighty Being, who rules over the universe, who presides in the councils of nations, and whose providential aids can supply every human defect, that His benediction may consecrate to the liberties and happiness of the people of the United States. . . . No people can be bound to acknowledge and adore the invisible hand which conducts the affairs of men more than the people of the United States. Every step by which they have advanced to the character of an independent nation seems to have been distinguished by some token of providential agency. . . . We ought to be no less persuaded that the propitious smiles of Heaven can never be expected on a nation that disregards the eternal rules of order and right, which Heaven itself has ordained.

49

With Malice Toward None

In the darkened upstairs room, the sixteenth President of the United States stared out into the winter night. His six-foot-four frame was bent, his hands clasped behind him, and every so often he would take a few measured paces over to the bed that had been his son William's, and then back to the window with its view of the distant Potomac, a silvery ribbon in the moonlight.

Somewhere across the river were the encampments of the Confederates, who, after their devastating victory at Bull Run the previous July, had been content to stand pat. And standing pat seemed to be the standing order of the day for the commander-in-chief of the Union forces, George McClelland, though he outnumbered his opponents by more than two to one. In the early months of 1862, the abolitionists were rabid at the delay, crying, "On to Richmond!", while a growing number of northern politicians were murmuring that the South could never be conquered. Pressure was mounting on the President to make peace now, let the South have its Confederacy, and put an end to further useless bloodshed. And newspapers of all persuasions had begun reviling him for everything that had gone wrong.

Yet Abraham Lincoln, more than any other President save Washington, perceived that God had a divine purpose for America — a purpose that could not come to pass, if the Union were not preserved. He understood the vision of a covenant nation, grounded on God's Word, that had compelled the Pilgrims and Puritans to come to the New World. He saw that vision as "something even more than National Independence. . .something that held out a great promise to all the people of the world to all times to come."

In February, he had articulated it further:

I am exceedingly anxious that this Union, this Constitution, and the liberties of the people shall be perpetuated in accordance with the original idea for which the struggle was made, and I shall be most happy indeed, if I shall be an humble instrument in the hands of the Almighty, and of this, His almost chosen people, for perpetuating the object of that great struggle.

*South view of
the White House.*

Lincoln at prayer.

But now that Union, not quite fourscore and seven years old, had been torn in half by bloody insurrection, and the two sides — one committed to slavery, the other free — were more set against reconciliation than ever. So much hurt had been inflicted on both sides, that the likelihood of the vision coming to pass seemed no more than a fading dream. Americans had always been an independent-minded people, and it appeared that they had made a series of willful choices that had thwarted God's plan for them, and were on the brink of losing what Lincoln termed "the last, best hope of earth."

By itself, the prospect of the Union lost forever would be enough to plunge even this extraordinary man into despair. Yet there was a still greater, personal grief weighing upon him this night, a grief that, instead of dissipating over the past few weeks, had grown more intense. For the little bed to his left would never again hold the form of his sleeping son. William had died at age eleven — William, who had been born just a year after the death of their second son, Edward. They had regarded William as a gift from a merciful God, but now he was gone, and the impact of this loss, coupled with the threat of losing the Union, had rendered the President inconsolable.

Alarmed at the widening chasm of despond that her husband was sinking into, Mary Lincoln sent for the Reverend Doctor Francis Vinton, rector of Trinity Church in New York.

Dr. Vinton arrived and came right to the point. "Do you remember that passage in the Gospels that says, 'God is not a God of the dead, but of the living; for all live unto Him'?"

The President nodded.

"Well, your son is *alive* — in Paradise."

"Alive?" Abraham Lincoln leapt to his feet, his knuckles whitening. "Alive! Surely you mock me!"

"No, sir, believe me; it is the most comforting doctrine of Christ Himself."

The President looked at his visitor, seeking his eyes and finding no guile there; only deep, steady conviction. With a sob, he came over and laid his head on Dr. Vinton's chest. The latter gently continued to expound the truth of life in the world to come, while his listener wept — not tears of grief, but tears of relief.

From that day forth, Lincoln's faith ceased to be intellectual and became profoundly personal. He was often seen carrying a Bible, and those closest to him recorded many moments of finding him in private prayer. Moreover, his entire outlook underwent a change, for, as Lincoln scholar Elton Trueblood put it, if God could not be defeated by the death of a little boy, then neither could He be defeated by a civil war. Lincoln stood taller after that, knowing that the burden was not on his shoulders but on God's. It was for him to seek God's will and to do it.

But that was not always easy when he knew that many of the strongest Confederate leaders were also men of prayer, or when he had callers and advisors telling him to take opposite actions, each convinced that they, and they alone, were speaking for God. More than once, the President graciously thanked these self-appointed messengers for their unbidden counsel, adding that when the Almighty told him the same thing, then he would most certainly act upon it.

"Yonder stands Jackson like a stonewall" — Thomas Jonathan "Stonewall" Jackson was one of the South's "praying generals." He prayed for his men and his officers every day, and as long as he lived, not one of his staff officers was killed or wounded.

Manassas Battlefield

In the meantime, he continued in earnest prayer and found an increasing measure of wisdom and discernment — both of which he would have great need of, for in August of '62, the Confederate forces under General Lee beat the Union army *again* at Bull Run, and were now threatening not only the Capitol, but an invasion of Pennsylvania.

As Washington had before him, Lincoln prayed for guidance, "in this time of crises, I was once again driven to my knees by the overwhelming conviction that I had no-where else to go." Later, he confided to his cabinet: "I made a solemn vow before God, that if General Lee was driven back from Pennsylvania, I would crown the result by the declaration of freedom to the slaves." The Emancipation Proclamation was something that the President had been contemplating for some time, and now, as Lee was finally stopped at Antietam, just short of the Pennsylvania border, and withdrew back across the Potomac, the President made good his vow, proclaiming all the slaves in the seceded states "Forever free."

Yet the war dragged on, and a little over a year later, at a windswept soldiers' grave-yard at Gettysburg, Lincoln gave further evidence of his unshakable determination to persevere through to the end, until the Union was reunited, and the vision's potential restored:

We here highly resolve that these dead shall not have died in vain; that this nation, under God, shall have a new birth of freedom; and that government of the people, by the people, for the people, shall not perish from the earth.

Another year of dreadful bloodshed passed, and the President came to see the prolongation of the nation's agony as a judgment of God upon them all, North and South, for having turned so far away from Him. By the time of his second Inaugural Address, on March 4, 1865, victory was at last in sight. The President looked to the future, when the suffering of both sides would be ended. He was adamant that there would be no vengeance exacted, no northern opportunists taking advantage of southern misfortune.

With malice toward none, with charity for all, with firmness in the right, as God gives us to see the right, let us strive to finish the work we are in, to bind up the nation's wounds, to care for him who shall have borne the battle and for his widow and orphan, to do all which may achieve and cherish a just and lasting peace among ourselves and with all nations.

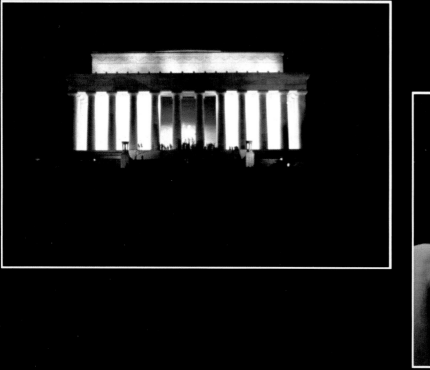

Lincoln Memorial

Had Lincoln lived, the aftermath of the war would have been radically different than it was. For he was determined that the sword would be buried, and North and South would dwell together as brothers, as God had always intended. But he did not live. Forty-one days after he spoke those words, on Good Friday he was cut down from behind by an assassin's bullet.

The vision which he held for America, in part came to pass, for the Union *was* preserved. Yet as a nation we have yet to fulfill that vision, and we have strayed far from the call that God had put upon us — so far, that if we do not soon turn back, we cannot expect His patience to last indefinitely. The point is, it is not too late to turn back. God's promise in II Chronicles is well known, but we have yet to take advantage of it. He has shown us the way: If we, His people who are called by His Name, will repent — if we will let the Holy Spirit convict us individually and corporately of the jealousy, divisiveness, and self-righteousness that have so separated and seek His face, then He will hear our prayers and heal our land.

And men like Abraham Lincoln, and all the other Americans who have given their lives for their country, will not have died in vain. And God will again shed His grace on America, from sea to shining sea.